The rural landscapes I have known have changed greatly
throughout the years. One thing remains. Farm families
continue to work and care for the land and the life they love
while providing food for a nation and world.

An excerpt from A Distance Traveled by Robert Buckner.

To farmers
and the families who farm

TORGI THE TRACTOR

Once Upon a Farm

Written and Illustrated by Robert Buckner

My story begins as a young farm tractor, fresh out of the factory. Farms and tractors like me were smaller than the tractors and farms of today. Now, imagine turning the pages of my book, and traveling back to another place and time. Are you ready for a visit to the farm? Let's go!

Before turning the page and beginning our tour, I want to share with you a note I found in the pages of my Log Book.

Leak in the radiator fixed — Torgi is cool again.
New plugs and wires — Torgi's got spark again.
New battery — all is well again.

Torgi, you are an amazing red tractor. You are a faithful tractor. Torgi, sometimes a large tractor is too big. And even today there are many jobs for tractors like you.

Welcome to spring Torgi, and another growing season!

Signed, *The Farmer*

Hi, welcome to the farm. Thanks for turning the page and stopping by for a visit. My name is Torgi, that's me, a bright red farm tractor pulling a load of hay. Hay is what my friends the cows and horses love to eat.

Let's hear it for the cows, and the horses too. Whoa, I don't see the horses, do you? They're here on the farm somewhere.

Torgi's pistons patter a throaty, "Ah, there you are horses, good day to you."

The horses reply, "And a good neigh to you too."

Shep, following behind, wags a farm dog tail to the greetings of the day.

I help the farmer with the field work, like plowing, cultivating, and so much more. My engine and gears provide the force, the torque it takes to pull the plow. And so the farmer named me Torgi! It's short for the torque we farm tractors need.

4

The farmer cares for the land and the animals on the farm. Listen. Do you hear the sounds of the farm as the barn cat meows and the cows' moo? The chickens cluck. The rooster crows. The donkey brays, "hee haw." The ducks quack. The goats' bleep. The sheep bah. The llama squeaks. The pigs' oink. The horses neigh. Shep, the farm dog, barks. Theirs are the voices of the farm animal choir, each member calling for the farmer's attention.

Once the plowing is done, and the soils are ready, the farmer and I plant corn seeds with the help of a planter. The farmer plants hay, a crop many of the animals need and enjoy. Both people and animals enjoy crops like corn, oats, soybeans and many more. Soon the plants will sprout, and summertime begins.

The farmer and I check out summer pastures on a beautiful blue-sky day.

We see eagles, birds, and the butterflies. The bees buzz, the butterflies flutter, and hummingbirds hover from flower to flower. I've heard the farmer say many times, "These are good signs that all is healthy and in balance."

9

Later, in the dusk of the day, we watch as a bat chases a moth. Like the bees, birds, and butterflies, bats are a farmer's friend too. They protect the leaves of the plants by eating the insects that attack them. These insects are a bat's favorite food.

Rain begins to fall, so it's off to the machine shed we go. The duck enjoys the shower, and Shep doesn't seem to mind. After the rain, the sun will shine. The plants are happy for both the sun and the rain.

14

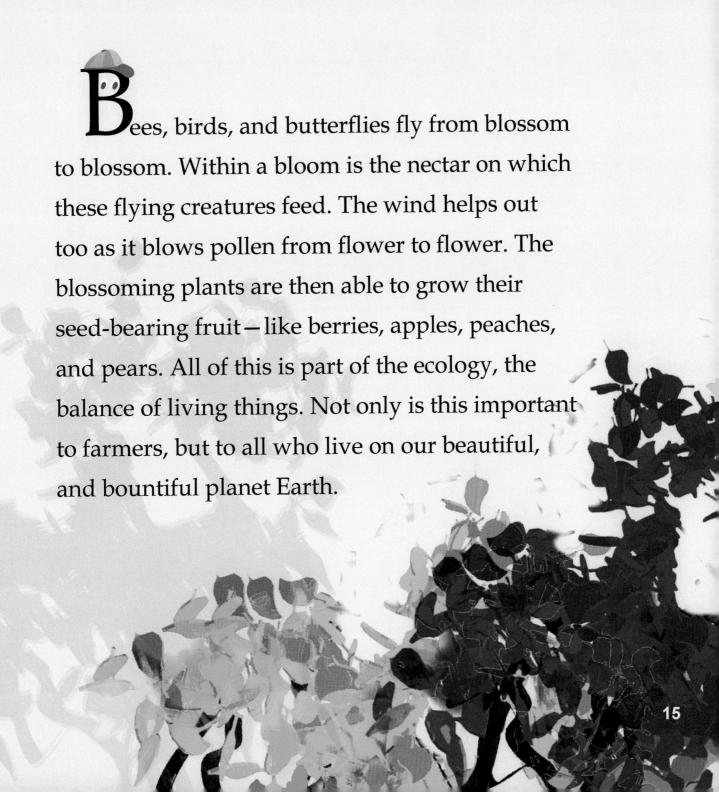

Bees, birds, and butterflies fly from blossom to blossom. Within a bloom is the nectar on which these flying creatures feed. The wind helps out too as it blows pollen from flower to flower. The blossoming plants are then able to grow their seed-bearing fruit—like berries, apples, peaches, and pears. All of this is part of the ecology, the balance of living things. Not only is this important to farmers, but to all who live on our beautiful, and bountiful planet Earth.

16

Fall's harvest moon is beautiful and bright. The farmer and I harvest a field of ripened grain. Tonight we work by the light of the moon. Farmers do their best to harvest the crops at the proper time. A bountiful harvest depends on timing.

One evening, the farmer entered the barn. It was empty. The farmer noticed the open door and a broken latch and wondered, "Where are the cows?" Help the farmer find the cows with this nursery rhyme hint.
"Little Boy Blue come blow your horn, the sheep are in the meadow, the cows are in the _ _ _ _."
Thanks for helping the farmer find the cows.

The farmer walks to a field of harvested corn. A rising moon greets the farmer, as do the cows playing hide and seek amid shocks of drying corn. A hay wagon and I rest nearby. "Ah," the farmer says, "I know just what to do."

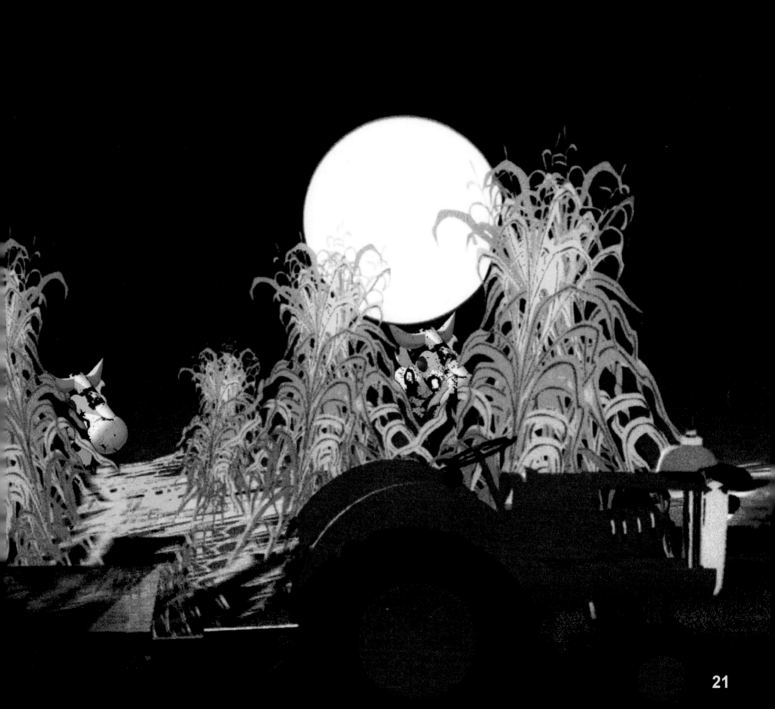

21

The farmer throws a shock of corn onto the wagon. "It's Torgi to the rescue," the farmer says, climbing onto my tractor seat. The cows follow alongside the wagon. As they munch on corn, the farmer sings a time-honored call for cows to come home. "Ca' Bossie, Ca' Bossie*..." Off to the barn, we go.

* Ca' is short for come. Bossie is a word for cow.

22

Through the open gate, an empty barn awaits the cows. Shep, the farm dog, knows what to do, and herds the cows safely into the barn. The farmer fixes the barn door latch, beds the cows with fresh new straw, and heads to the farmhouse for a good night's sleep.

The next morning the farmer milks the cows and goats and tends to all the animals on the farm. With the morning chores finished, the farmer walks to the farmhouse, opens the door, and enters the warmth of the kitchen. There on the table are eggs from the hens, milk from the cows, cheese from the goats, bacon from the pigs, and a bowl of the farmer's favorite cereal which is a gift of the fields. And the farmer gives thanks!

Welcome To the
FARMERS' MARKET

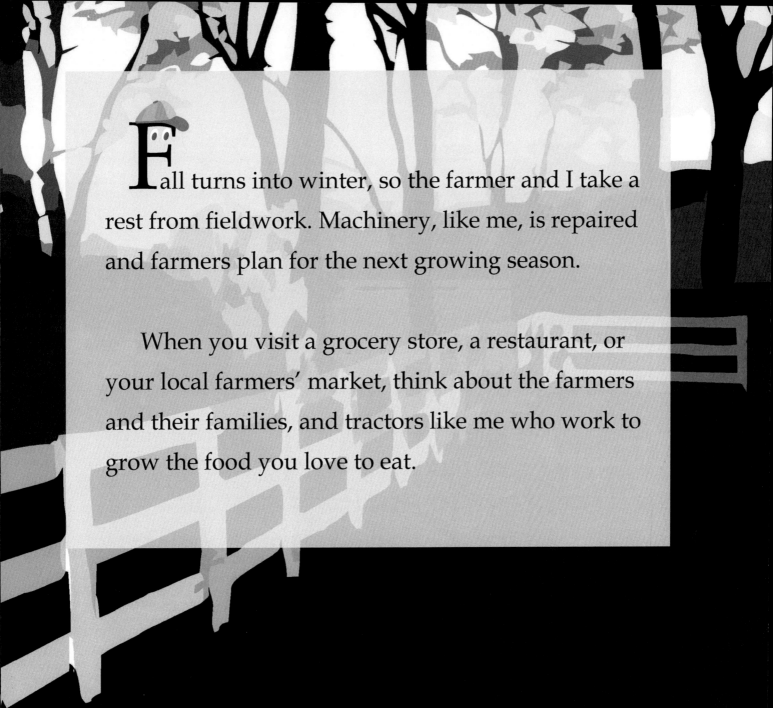

Fall turns into winter, so the farmer and I take a rest from fieldwork. Machinery, like me, is repaired and farmers plan for the next growing season.

When you visit a grocery store, a restaurant, or your local farmers' market, think about the farmers and their families, and tractors like me who work to grow the food you love to eat.

Winter's snowflakes fall from the sky, coloring the countryside white. The farmer and I plow the snow from the driveway. Winter is a time of rest for the fields as they sleep beneath their blanket of snow. Come spring, all of us will be rested and ready for the beginning of another busy growing season.

Thanks for stopping by for a tour of the farm. Shep, the farm dog, misses you already. How quickly time passes when we take the time to read a book and turn its pages.

Good-bye now. Always good to see you. Stop by anytime.

To readers of this book:

Our precious Earth is a diversified mix of many peoples, species of plants, birds, insects, and animals specific to our local surroundings. Ecology is a name given to the interaction of living organisms and all that is a part of our environment. Every living creature plays an essential role in this ecology.

Years ago, people settled, on the land, clearing trees and grasses to prepare the soil for farming. Farmers planted a variety of seeds which grew into thriving plants. These plants provided much-needed food for farm families. Later, more people came, and towns and cities sprang up. Farm families were able to buy the goods and services they needed to make their lives easier and their farms more productive.

Farm tractors are just one of the many goods manufactured by people who live and work in the city. Tractors and new methods of farming give farmers the ability to provide more food for more people. The food we buy at our grocery stores come from farms. Just as a balanced diet is vital to our health, a balanced ecology is essential to the earth and all living things.

About the author and this book: Robert Buckner works as an artist and writer. Having spent time as a youth on the farms of relatives and friends, the author and illustrator bring to life the story of "Torgi the Tractor." Having sat on a drawing board far too long, Torgi is now happy to present through the pages of this book, the importance of farms, and care for the environment.

Robert Buckner, artist and author spends time with Herc while on a visit to Carol's farm.

Other books by Robert Buckner include:

"Sail On, Little Whee"—The story begins with the building of a sailboat in the machine shed on a farm. Left alone in a field the sailboat dreams of sailing. Eventually, the sailboat, Little Whee, makes its way to the ocean. Along the way, the sailboat finds adventure and makes new friends.

"Red's Caboose" and "I Built a Snowman" are books illustrated by Robert Buckner, authored by Julane Severson.

For more information visit us online:

Robert's site: www.creativedreamings.com

Julane's site: www.friendchipfarm.com

Made in the USA
Lexington, KY
05 June 2018